Helping Young Children to Speak With Confidence

ACKNOWLEDGEMENTS

Written by: Ros Bayley, Lynn Broadbent & Andrina Flinders

Illustrated by: Peter Scott

Produced & Published by: Lawrence Educational
PO Box 532
Cambridge, CB1 0BX, UK

© Lawrence Educational 2004

ISBN: 978-1-903670-33-0

All rights reserved. This book is sold subject to the condition that it shall not, by way of trade or otherwise, be lent, hired out or otherwise circulated without the prior consent of Lawrence Educational in any form of binding or cover other than that in which it is published.

No part of this publication may be reproduced, stored in a retrieval system, or transmitted, in any form of by any means, electronic, mechanical, photocopying, recording or otherwise, without the permission of Lawrence Educational.

INTRODUCTION

Good speaking and listening skills are at the heart of the learning process, and without them, children are at a real disadvantage. In fact, when you look at all the things that speaking and listening enables, it becomes really clear why early years practitioners attach so much importance to this important aspect of children's development.

Speaking and listening enables us to:

* share ideas
* try out new ideas
* develop other's ideas
* ask questions
* clarify or ask for information
* participate

* share experiences
* defend a point of view
* learn to take turns
* answer questions
* reflect on experiences
* build confidence

'Helping Young Children To Speak With Confidence' has been designed to assist practitioners in facilitating children's development in this vital area. The publication revolves around an appealing chimpanzee called Kofi, who the children seem to take to immediately. Kofi has the capacity to engage them at an emotional level, and as we all know, when the emotions are engaged, the learning is always deeper. Below is an example of how Kofi was introduced to the children in the pilot schools. However, this does not mean that you have to introduce him in exactly the same way. You may well have some very creative ideas of your own, and that is absolutely fine!

INTRODUCING KOFI

Bring Kofi into the classroom in a box, or wrapped in a blanket so that the children cannot see him. Explain that when you were at the airport you found Kofi lying on the conveyor belt at baggage reclaim. Go on to tell them about how he was all by himself and that no-one seemed to want him. Tell the children that he looked very worried and lonely so you tried to find out who he belonged to, but that nobody knew anything about him. If you are able to take photographs of this process it will really add to the excitement. (Alternatively, show the children the photographs printed here).

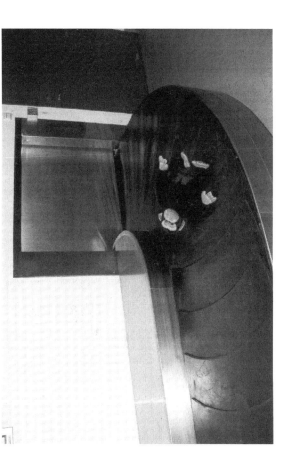

Finally, explain that you bought him home with you thinking that the children would look after him. You will now have set the scene for the games and activities in the book, which are all based on the premise that Kofi needs their help in understanding lots of things.

USING THE ACTIVITIES

Prior to using the activities with the children pass Kofi around so that they can all meet him. Talk with them about how a good speaker behaves and introduce them to the groundrules at the front of the book. (These should be photocopied and displayed on the wall, so that they can be referred to at the beginning and end of sessions).

The activities do follow a logical progression, but there is no particular way in which to use them. Flick through the book and pick out the activities that are most suitable for the children you are working with. As many of the activities are circle games, they will probably need to be planned into your daily routine, but you will find that there are some that can be carried out at odd moments or at transition times. In the main, any resources required should be reasonably easy to find and the instructions have been written as concisely as possible to aid busy practitioners. You will probably also find that you will adapt some of the activities, and add to them by inventing your own. But however you decide to use this book we sincerely hope it helps you with your speaking and listening work and that you have fun!

A good speaker:

Looks at their audience.

A good speaker:

Waits for their turn.

A good speaker:

Talks clearly.

A good speaker:

Thinks before they talk.

ACTIVITY 1

Greetings!

Purpose:
This is a perfect activity to use with children after introducing Kofi, as it gives them the opportunity to introduce themselves to him.

Resources:
None required.

Process:
1. Sit the children in a circle.
2. Pass round an object and let the children take turns to introduce themselves when holding it.
3. Then ask the children to continue passing the object round as you play music. When the music stops the child holding the object asks to swap places with a friend. Encourage them to speak at a suitable volume so that their friend can hear and use the talk line, "I would like to swap with……"
4. This activity can be extended or adapted to include greetings in other languages, such as Urdu, French or Spanish.

ACTIVITY 2

Home, Sweet Home

Purpose:
This activity has been designed to help children begin to build a relationship with Kofi, by taking responsibility for making him a new home and thinking about what he might need.

Resources:
Empty boxes, tubes, paper plates, plastic cups and other recycled materials.

Process:
1. Sit the children in a circle.
2. Explain that now Kofi has come to stay with them he is going to need a home.
3. Pass an object around and encourage the children to use the talk line "Kofi's home will need a ……". Model the talk line first. If a child passes, return to them at the end and offer them a further opportunity to speak. Some children will have the same/similar ideas, but that's fine.
4. You could also record their ideas on a white board and then during the week children could take turns in helping to make Kofi a home. This could then be displayed and used to keep Kofi safe.

ACTIVITY 3

Favourites

Purpose:
This activity has been designed to build children's confidence by giving them the opportunity to talk about familiar things.

Resources:
None required.

Process:
1. Sit the children in a circle.
2. Explain that Kofi wants to find out about their favourite things. Model the talk line.... "My favourite TV programme/story/colour/animal/food is……."
3. Pass an object around the circle and let the children tell Kofi about their favourite things.
4. Encourage them to speak at a suitable volume and use the talk line you have modelled.
5. This activity can be repeated a number of times by changing the talk line.

ACTIVITY 4

Friends

Purpose:
This activity has been designed to get the children talking about their friends.

Resources:
None required.

Process:
1. Sit the children in a circle.
2. Explain that yesterday Kofi found your watch on the floor. Tell the children that it is a very special watch that your friend gave you for your birthday. Further explain that Kofi doesn't know what a friend is and that he needs the children to help him to understand.
3. Pass an object around and ask the children to tell Kofi what friends are and talk about the sorts of things you can do with them. Some children may choose to pass, but you can return to them once everyone has had a go and offer them a further opportunity to speak.
4. Encourage them to speak at a suitable volume.
5. Then explain to them that Kofi would like to know who their friends are and why they like them. Model the talk line "My friend is .... and I like her because ...." Pass an object around the circle and let the children tell Kofi about their friends.

© Lawrence Educational   Helping Young Children Speak With Confidence

ACTIVITY 5

Retell A Story

Purpose:
This activity has been designed to help children recall familiar/unfamiliar stories.

Resources:
A familiar text.

Process:
1. Sit the children together on the carpet. Explain that Kofi wants to come to story time. However, when you go to fetch him from his home he's not there. Instead there is a note, which says, "popped to the shops, but don't worry I'll be back for story time".
2. Sit down and wait a short while for Kofi to arrive, and then explain to the children that you can't wait any longer and that you'll have to start without him.
3. Read the story to the children discussing the characters and events.
4. Arrange for a colleague to knock the door and bring in Kofi just as you finish the story.
5. Explain that he has missed the story, but that if he listens carefully the children might tell him what happened.
6. Explain to the children that you are going to try to retell the story in the correct order not missing anything out.
7. Pass an object around and let the children take turns to retell the story. They may need a lot of support the first time they do this. But Kofi could be late for story time again!

© Lawrence Educational

Helping Young Children Speak With Confidence

ACTIVITY 6

Talent Contest

Purpose:
This activity has been designed to help build children's confidence when speaking in front of each other. It also encourages them to evaluate each other's work.

Resources:
No resources.

Process:
1. Sit the children together on the carpet. Explain that they are going to take part in a talent show. Tell them that they can stand up and show Kofi and the rest of the children anything they think they are good at. Remind them that everybody is good at something. You may wish to provide some examples of the things they could do e.g. sing a song/nursery rhyme, count forwards/backwards to ten, jump/run on the spot, dance etc.
2. The children may need time to prepare, so the talent show activity could be introduced just before child initiated learning to allow time to practise. Encourage shy children to join larger groups and remind them of talents that they could show off.
3. If this activity is repeated on a number of occasions the children's confidence will grow and shy children will be more likely to join in.
4. This activity can also be extended to include judge's comments. As each acts finishes the children can be encouraged to talk about what they **liked** and why they **liked** it. This should be a positive experience that boosts the performer's confidence and develops language skills.

© Lawrence Educational   Helping Young Children Speak With Confidence

ACTIVITY 7

Snap Shots

Purpose:
This activity has been designed to develop children's communication skills by giving them the opportunity to talk about a photograph brought from home.

Resources:
Children's photographs of family, special occasions or places bought from home.

Process:
1. Sit the children in a circle. Explain that Kofi is feeling homesick and that they are going to cheer him up by telling him about their friends and family.

2. Explain that the first thing they are going to do is to introduce the person in the photograph by using the talk line, "This is my .... and his/her name is ...." Model this using your own photograph.

3. The children then take it in turns to introduce the person in their photograph.

4. Explain that Kofi would like to know more about these people. Model the second talk line "I like them because..........." The children then take turns to use the second talk line.

5. You may feel that this activity could be extended to include other talk lines.

6. This activity can also be repeated using photographs of special occasions, places or photographs of special activities.

© Lawrence Educational   Helping Young Children Speak With Confidence

ACTIVITY 8

Playing With Our Voices

Purpose:
This activity has been designed to raise children's awareness of the need to look at the listener and speak with clarity and at an appropriate volume.

Resources:
A recording device.

Process:
1. Sit the children together on the carpet. Explain that we can make our voices do lots of different things and that this is called an impression. Invite them to take turns to do an impression of an animal, a car, a door slamming or a firework etc. Encourage the other children to try to guess what is being impersonated.
2. You might try singing 'Old McDonald Had a Farm' encouraging the children to use their voices to make animal/tractor/creaking door noises. Record the song, then play it back so that they can hear all the different voices they made.
3. The activity can then be extended so that the children can experiment with volume and direction. Ask them to choose their favourite nursery rhyme and to say it quietly/loudly etc. You may need to demonstrate this. Discuss which one they could hear the best and talk about the implications for when we talk to each other.
4. Next, ask a child to say a nursery rhyme facing in different directions (up in the air, against a wall or towards the floor etc). Again, discuss the implications for when we talk to each other.

© Lawrence Educational   Helping Young Children Speak With Confidence   8

ACTIVITY 9

What's This For?

Purpose:
This activity has been designed to get children thinking about the information they need to include when they are providing an explanation. It uses objects from around the setting and can be repeated using different objects. For example, objects from the kitchen, bathroom or garden shed.

Resources:
A selection of objects, e.g. pencil, felt pen, paint brush, puppet, spade, lego brick, sticker, book, rolling pin etc. Objects could be chosen from a role-play area you have recently set up, or linked to a topic of current interest.

Process:
1. Sit the children in a circle. Explain that Kofi has been looking around the classroom and that he has found lots of objects that he doesn't know what they are. Tell them that he is wondering if they could explain what each object is called, what it is for and where it is kept. Choose an object and model giving the relevant information.
2. Pass the object around the circle and let the children take turns to add to the explanation. Encourage them to talk in sentences and return to those who pass to offer them a further opportunity to speak.

ACTIVITY 10

How Do You Put This On?

Purpose:
This activity has been designed to get children thinking about how to give instructions.

Resources:
A selection of clothing.

Process:
1. Sit the children in a circle. Explain that Kofi has found the clothes and that he doesn't know what they are for.
2. Choose a child to select a piece of clothing and tell Kofi what it is for.
3. They can then pass the item of clothing around the circle and take it in turns to add further pieces of information, such as where you wear it and why.
4. This activity can be extended to include talking about the order in which items of clothing need to be put on e.g. socks then shoes etc.

ACTIVITY 11

Express Yourself

Purpose:
This activity has been designed to encourage children to talk with expression.

Resources:
A selection of empty food packages.

Process:
1. Sit the children in a circle and explain that when we talk we show our emotions. Give them some demonstrations and see if they can guess how you are feeling, e.g. excited, scared or sad.
2. Place the empty food packages in the middle of the circle and explain to the children that they are going to choose a package and express how they feel about it. Model the talk line "I like/dislike ………. They are …(yummy/yucky)……."
3. The children then take turns to choose a package and express how they feel about it.
4. This activity can then be finished by reading a story with lots of expression. Encouraging the children to notice how the use of expression makes the story more enjoyable.

ACTIVITY 12

Phone For a Take-Away

Purpose:
This activity has been designed to increase the children's awareness of the technology we use when communicating.

Resources:
A telephone and take away menu (or you could choose to ring McDonalds!)

Process:
1. Sit the children in a circle and explain that Kofi is hungry. Pretend to ring for a take away and order Kofi some food from the menu. Use the talk line, "Hello, I would like to order ...., thank you".
2. Ask the children if they would like to order something, then pass around the phone and the menu and let each child order their food.
3. This activity can be repeated and the children can order their Christmas presents from Argos etc.

© Lawrence Educational

Helping Young Children Speak With Confidence

ACTIVITY 13

This Is My Work And This Is How I Did It

Purpose:
This activity has been designed to provide the children with an opportunity to talk about their work and the process they engaged in as they did it. It can be used during plenary sessions on a regular basis.

Resources:
A few pieces of children's work.

Process:
1. This activity would be very lengthy if all the children had a go at talking about their work. Consequently it is more beneficial if done on a regular basis using groups of children. Done this way, each child will have more time to talk and over a period of time the children's confidence and skill at explaining will develop.
2. Sit the children in a circle. Those children who are showing their work then take it in turns to talk about what they have done, how they did it, what they have learned and how they feel about it. As the children's skill at talking about their own work develops you can encourage their explanation to become lengthier. To begin with you will need to model the process, encouraging the children to notice how you introduced the item and how you proceeded with your explanation.

© Lawrence Educational

Helping Young Children Speak With Confidence

13

ACTIVITY 14

The Mystery Object

Purpose:
This activity has been designed to encourage prediction.

Resources:
A selection of familiar objects, e.g. a fork, a pencil sharpener, a bar of soap, an empty packet of crisps, a board rubber, a toy car etc. and a feely bag.

Process:
1. Sit the children in a circle and explain that Kofi has placed an object in the feely bag and that he wants them to try and guess what it is. Model the talk line "I think it is a ………. because……."
2. Then pass the feely bag around the circle so that each child can predict what is inside using the given talk line. You may wish to encourage the children to use their different senses or wait to see how they investigate the bag. Thinking of reasons for their prediction may take time to develop, but the more the children play the game the better they will become.

© Lawrence Educational

Helping Young Children Speak With Confidence

ACTIVITY 15

Hide and Seek

Purpose:
This activity has been designed to encourage the children to think about how to give instructions. It will also help them to practise positional language.

Resources:
A soft toy.

Process:
1. Sit the children together on the carpet. Ask them if they have ever played the game Hide and Seek. If they have, ask them to explain the game to Kofi, who has never played it.
2. Explain to the children that they are going to play the game a little differently. Choose two children; one child to hide the toy and a second child to help find it. The first child hides the toy then gives instructions to the second child to enable them to find it.
3. Encourage the children to think about how many instructions are needed. Can they enable the other person to find the toy with just one clear instruction? Model giving the instructions first so that the children understand the game.

© Lawrence Educational

Helping Young Children Speak With Confidence

ACTIVITY 16

Guess Who?

Purpose:
This activity has been designed to provide opportunities for the children to ask questions and think about how to phrase them.

Resources:
None needed

Process:
1. Sit the children together on the carpet and explain that Kofi has a game for them to play called 'Guess Who?' Model how to play the game. Choose a child's name and write it down on a piece of paper, (when children do this they can whisper the name to you and you can write it down for them). Next the children ask you questions to try to guess whose name you have written down. E.g. is it a boy or girl? Has this person got long hair or short hair? Is this person wearing trainers? etc. Initially, it may be helpful to get another adult to play the game with you. Once children have seen it modelled a few times they soon get the hang of it!

ACTIVITY 17

Let's Do It Together

Purpose:
This activity has been designed to provide opportunities for children to work collaboratively.

Resources:
Building blocks for constructing a tower or a large piece of paper and felt pens for drawing a picture.

Process:
1. For this activity you can choose whether the children work collaboratively to build a model or draw a picture.
2. Sit the children together on the carpet and explain that they are going to work together to build a model or draw a picture. Tell them that Kofi wants to know what they are doing, so each time they make a move they need to explain it to him. Model this using the talk line, "I'm going to draw/build a ......". The children then volunteer to takes turns to work collaboratively.

ACTIVITY 18

Classify This

Purpose:
This activity has been designed to encourage the children to think about how to sort objects or pictures.

Resources:
A selection of objects or pictures.

Process:
1. Sit the children in a circle on the carpet. Explain that Kofi has collected lots of objects/pictures in his bag and that he wants them to help him to sort them.
2. Empty the bag into the middle of the circle. Model how to sort the objects and how to explain the criteria you have used. The children can then follow your lead. E.g. "I'm going to put this spade over here because it belongs in the sand".
3. The children then take turns to classify the remaining objects/pictures.

ACTIVITY 19

Change Seats

Purpose
This activity builds on 'Greetings' and is designed to give individual children the opportunity to give directions to the rest of the group.

Resources
None required

Process
1. Sit the children on chairs in a circle and explain that you are going to play a game that is going to require them to be very truthful! Further explain that as Kofi cannot speak for himself one of them will have to take responsibility for him.

2. Tell the children that you are going to use the talk line. 'Change seats if you............' (add to the line as you wish, e.g. ...'if you have got a dog' .... 'if you have got a brother' ...... 'if you like chocolate' etc.)

3. The children listen carefully and change seats accordingly.

4. Once they have seen you model the process they take it in turns to direct the group.

5. Encourage the rest of the children to give positive feedback, e.g. 'You spoke really clearly.'

© Lawrence Educational

Helping Young Children Speak With Confidence

ACTIVITY 20

Who's Who?

Purpose
This activity is designed to give the children the opportunity to share what they know about key people in your setting.

Resources
A set of photographs

Process
1. Explain to the children that you have got a set of photographs of people that work in their setting, and that they are going to tell Kofi all about these people.
2. Select a photograph and model how to share information about the person in the photograph.
3. Pass the photograph on to the child sitting next to you so that they can add something to the information you have given. If they don't have any information to share they pass the photograph on to the next person.
4. When there is no more information to share, select another photograph and begin the process again

© Lawrence Educational   Helping Young Children Speak With Confidence

ACTIVITY 21

How Would You Greet Them?

Purpose

This activity is designed to help children to understand that we use language differently in different contexts.

Resources

The same set of photographs that are used for the 'Who's Who?' activity with some further photographs added. E.g. pictures of the children's parents, brothers and sisters, plus pictures of footballers, pop stars, television personalities etc.

Process

1. Explain to the children that we greet people differently, depending on who they are and our relationship with them, but that Kofi needs them to help him to know how to do this.

2. Sit the children in a circle and model the ways in which you would say hello to the various people in the picture.

3. Pass an object (or Kofi) around the circle and on the given signal, the child with the object selects a photograph and tells Kofi how they would greet this person. E.g. this is a picture of Jamie's brother and I would greet him by saying, 'Hi Jamie, how are you mate?' or this is a picture of Jamie's mum and I would greet her by saying, 'Hello Mrs. Davis.' Invite the rest of the children to comment on whether they would do it any differently.

4. Repeat the process using a different picture.

© Lawrence Educational

Helping Young Children Speak With Confidence

ACTIVITY 22

What Happens Here?

Purpose
This activity is designed to give the children an opportunity to share information about places in the setting and in the local area.

Resources
Photographs of parts of the setting and places in the local area.

Process
1. Explain to the children that Kofi needs to know about what happens in the places shown in the photographs, e.g. the secretary's office.
2. Model how to give information about one of the photographs and then pass it on to the child sitting next to you and ask if they can add to the information you have given.
3. Pass the photograph on around the circle, and when there is no more information to add, select another photograph and repeat the process.

ACTIVITY 23

The Invitation

Purpose
This activity is designed to give the children an opportunity to give advice and information in relation to a birthday party.

Resources
An invitation card

Process
1. Explain to the children that Kofi has received an invitation to a birthday party. Pass the card around for them all to see.
2. Further explain that although Kofi is excited about the invitation, he is also a bit nervous, as he has never been to a birthday party before. Tell them that he wants to know what he should take with him and what sort of things will happen when he gets there.
3. Model how to give Kofi this information and then pass an object around the circle and let the children take turns to add to the information you have already given.

ACTIVITY 24

Where Can You Buy It?

Purpose
This activity is designed to enable the children to share information about the shops in the local area.

Resources
A set of photographs of shops, supermarkets, garages etc. in the local area and a shopping list.

Process
1. Explain to the children that Kofi needs to go shopping. Tell them that he has got a list of all the things that he wants to buy but he is not sure which shops sell which things.
2. Lay the photographs out in the middle of the circle and taking the first thing from Kofi's list, model how to give him the information he needs. For example, 'Kofi, if you want to get a toothbrush you need to go to the chemists'. Then, show Kofi the photograph of the appropriate shop.
3. Pass an object around the circle and let the children take turns to tell Kofi where he can get all of the things he needs.

© Lawrence Educational

Helping Young Children Speak With Confidence

ACTIVITY 25

The Daily Routine

Purpose
This activity is structured to enable the children to think about and give information about the daily routine of the setting.

Resources
Cards showing the various aspects of the daily routine, e.g. activity time, snack time, outside time, welcome time etc.

Process
1. Tell the children that Kofi keeps getting confused about the daily routine and is not sure about what happens at various stages of the day.
2. Explain to them that they are going to take each aspect of the daily routine in order, and tell Kofi as much as they can about that part of the day.
3. Model how to do this and then pass an object around the circle and let the children take turns to add to the information you have already given.

ACTIVITY 26

Kofi's Backpack

Purpose
This activity is designed to provide opportunities for the children to speculate about where a variety of things might have come from.

Resources
A variety of objects to put into Kofi's backpack or case, such as a pebble, a key, a pair of swimming goggles, etc.

Process
1. Pack the objects into Kofi's backpack and explain to the children that Kofi has been out for a walk and that he has collected lots of things. Further explain that he wants them to try to guess where he has been. Model how to do this by providing a talk line, e.g. 'This is a .... and I think Kofi has been to .... because.........'.
2. Pass an object around the circle and on a signal from you the child holding the object draws an item from Kofi's collection and speculates on where he might have been. Invite the rest of the children to add their thoughts to what has already been said.
3. Once the children have got the idea of the game, make the objects more challenging

© Lawrence Educational

Helping Young Children Speak With Confidence

26

ACTIVITY 27

Kofi's Present

Purpose
This activity enables the children to make a prediction and explain the thinking behind their prediction.

Resources
A present

Process
1. Explain that Kofi has received a present and that before he opens it he wants them to try to guess what is inside it.
2. Show the children Kofi's present and pass it around the circle so that they feel the weight etc.
3. Model how to make a prediction, e.g. 'I think Kofi has been given .... and I think this because'.
4. Pass the parcel around again and as it goes around encourage each child to make a prediction. Don't worry if someone says the same thing as the person before them.
5. Once everyone has had a turn, open the present and see how many people made a correct prediction.

© Lawrence Educational

Helping Young Children Speak With Confidence

27

ACTIVITY 28

The Boot Sale

Purpose
This activity is designed to give the children opportunities for speculation and explanation.

Resources
A selection of objects the purpose of which may not be immediately evident to the children, e.g. a tyre pressure gauge, a sink plunger, a wire whisk, a garlic press, a toasting fork etc.

Process
1. Sit the children in a circle and one by one, pass the items around for them to look at.
2. Explain that at the weekend Kofi went to a car boot sale and bought lots of things that he liked the look of. Further explain that now that he has got them he has no idea what they are for and that he wants the children to help him.
3. Pass one of the items around the circle and let the children explain what they think it is used for. If they have no idea they pass the item onto the child sitting next to them.
4. When no more information can be offered, repeat the process with another item.

© Lawrence Educational

Helping Young Children Speak With Confidence

ACTIVITY 29

How Do You Get There?

Purpose
This activity is designed to provide an opportunity for the children to give directions.

Resources
Some photographs of places in your setting and the immediate environment.

Process
1. Explain to the children that Kofi keeps getting lost because he cannot remember how to get to places.
2. Generate ideas for what you could do to help him, and then model directions to one of the places featured in your photographs.
3. Select another photograph and then pass an object around the circle and let the children take turns to give Kofi directions.

© Lawrence Educational — Helping Young Children Speak With Confidence

ACTIVITY 30

Who Does It Belong To?

Purpose

Resources

A bag that has been packed with a variety of personal possessions that lead to someone's identity, e.g. a gardener, a builder, a cook, a footballer, a postman, a storybook character, or a person who works in your setting (if you can persuade them to lend you some things!)

Process

1. Explain to the children that Kofi has found a bag that has been left in the outside area and that he wants to find out who it belongs to.
2. Take an item as an example and model the talk line, E.g. 'this is a trowel, so I think this bag belongs to someone who likes gardening.'
3. Pass the item onto the child sitting next to you to see if they wish to add anything to what you have already said.
4. When there is nothing further to be said take another item from the bag.
5. Keep going until you have identified who the bag belongs to.

© Lawrence Educational Helping Young Children Speak With Confidence

Case Study
Grove School, Birmingham

Introducing Kofi
Introducing Kofi was a special session. I told the children the story of how I found him, whilst keeping him hidden in a box. We talked about who might be inside and what may have happened to them. I had even managed to get some photographs of Kofi inside an airport. We then discussed and built a house for him and explained daily routines.

Playing the games
Some children found the activities very challenging, but the more we played them the more progress they made. Wherever possible I made cross-curricular links and used the games as warm ups/plenary to lessons. For example, links were made to Mathematics (hide and seek positional language), Understanding the World (mystery objects linked to topics) and Literacy (retelling stories). I also found that the activities covered many of the Communication and Language objectives and therefore by playing them w ewere planning for S&L provision.

When playing the games the children used a plastic banana as a talking stick, this helped control behaviour because children talked only when holding it. We also used other objects such as mobile phones and microphones. The posters were displayed in the classroom and referred to each time we began a game, this reminded children of what makes a good speaker and therefore what is expected of them.

When playing the games, I found the role of the classroom assistant very useful. Firstly, they were able to help model the activities and talk alongside the children. Also, some of the activities provided the opportunity for my classroom assistant to make observations that were then used to inform the EYFS Profiles.

We even took Kofi on our school trip. When we returned, we talked about the day and made a scrapbook of photographs that the children could return to in their own time.

The children also took turns in taking Kofi home. When they returned with him the next day, they could talk about what they got up to the previous night.

In using Kofi we have had lots of fun and undertook many quality speaking and listening sessions. I also feel that my children now have a far greater understanding of what makes a good speaker and therefore understand what they need to do. The children loved Kofi and his presence motivated them to talk.

Andrina Flinders

We hope you have found this publication useful. Other books in our 'Helping Young Children' series are:

Helping Young Children with STEADY BEAT	978-1-903670-26-2
Helping Young Children with PHONOLOGICAL AWARENESS	978-1-903670-73-6
Helping Young Children with NUMERACY	978-1-903670-20-0
Helping Young Children with PHONICS	978-1-903670-13-2
Helping Young Children LEARN TO READ	978-1-903670-32-3
Helping Young Children to SPEAK WITH CONFIDENCE	978-1-903670-33-0
Helping Young Children to LISTEN	978-1-903670-04-0
Helping Young Children to CONCENTRATE	978-1-903670-29-3
Helping Young Children to COME TO THEIR SENSES	978-1-903670-57-6
Helping Young Children to IMAGINE	978-1-903670-12-5
Helping Young Children to THINK CREATIVELY	978-1-903670-14-9
Helping Young Children to LEARN THROUGH MOVEMENT	978-1-903670-34-7
Helping Young Children with PSE through story	978-1-903670-45-3
Helping Young Children to ASK QUESTIONS	978-1-903670-36-1

For further information about these and our other publications, visit our website:

www.LawrenceEducational.co.uk